Praise for *The Knot of My T*

T0032309

"In Zehra Naqvi's *The Knot of My Tongu*[...] prayer to be understood, Musa's prayer for witness, animates these poems, reiterates the prayer, and meets it with action. Silence and storytelling form a lush tapestry, a tender and rigorous interrogation, tightly knotted in the long history of women, beginning here in these poems to unknot."

—Safia Elhillo, author of *Girls That Never Die*

"Zehra Naqvi knows the *poetry of rain*. Remembering *barish*, for baba, the poet has walked continents away, still singing the intimacies and mythologies of family and home. After the storm, out beyond moments and rooms, Naqvi determines the form, reads her own body, and carries the day with this shining debut—elegant and unforgettable."

—Cecily Nicholson, author of *Harrowings*

"'Here in the after / how do I give myself form?' Zehra Naqvi's debut book of poems is a steady reckoning with inheritance: a contention of private pain against rituals of collective mourning that venerate female prophetic voices of witness from Hajar to Zainab. *The Knot of My Tongue* moves through forms of pilgrimage both embodied (as the Arba'in walk from Najaf to Karbala) and as an introspective reclamation of the will, the splendid emergence of the poetic self."

—Rahat Kurd, author of *Cosmophilia*

"It's clear to me that Zehra Naqvi's long-awaited debut is a future classic. *The Knot of My Tongue* weaves matriarchal elegy and triumph into an absolutely riveting, multilingual devotion that echoes long after the last page. This is a text I will return to and learn from again and again."

—Leah Horlick, author of *Moldovan Hotel*

"In the tradition of the many great poet-revolutionaries, Naqvi deploys language like a tool: as a call to action, testament against injustice, and container for ancestral memories. More than that, however, she guides us, expertly and with great vulnerability, through the spaces between words towards those truths that are only found beyond the pale of language."

—Irfan Ali, author of *Accretion*

THE KNOT
OF MY
TONGUE

Poems

ZEHRA NAQVI

McClelland & Stewart

McClelland & Stewart and colophon are registered trademarks of
Penguin Random House Canada Limited.

Published simultaneously in the United States of America.

Library and Archives Canada Cataloguing in Publication data is available upon request.

ISBN: 978-0-7710-1493-2
ebook ISBN: 978-0-7710-1134-4

Cover design by Talia Abramson
Cover images: (details) The Textile Museum Collection, Washington, D.C., 6.40, Acquired by
George Hewitt Myers in 1930, Photography by Breton Littlehales; The Textile Museum
Collection, Washington, D.C., R63.00.12, Acquired by George Hewitt Myers, Photography by
Breton Littlehales; The Textile Museum Collection, Washington, D.C., 1.83, Gift of Mrs. Hoffman
Philip, Photography by Renee Comet; The Textile Museum Collection, Washington, D.C., 6.140,
Acquired by George Hewitt Myers in 1948, Photography by Breton Littlehales; The Textile
Museum Collection, Washington, D.C., 1985.57.44, Gift of Alice Bradley Sheldon; collected by
Mary Hastings Bradley, Photography by Breton Littlehales; The Textile Museum Collection,
Washington, D.C., 1972.29.2, Gift of Ronald Harvey Goodman, Photography by Breton
Littlehales; The Textile Museum Collection, Washington, D.C., 6.118, Acquired by George
Hewitt Myers in 1947, Photography by Breton Littlehales; The Textile Museum Collection,
Washington, D.C., 1963.36.11, Acquired by George Hewitt Myers, Photography by Breton
Littlehales; The Textile Museum Collection, Washington, D.C., r33.26.1, Acquired by George
Hewitt Myers in 1940, Photography by Breton Littlehales; Textile Fragment, The Met, 52.20.22,
Purchase, Joseph Pulitzer Bequest, 1952; Carpet with Palm Trees, Ibexes, and Birds, The Met,
17.190.858, Gift of J. Pierpont Morgan, 1917; The 'Nigde' Carpet, The Met, 56.217, Gift of Joseph V.
McMullan, 1956; (birds) tigerstrawberry / Getty Images; mentalmind / Shutterstock

Typeset in Perpetua by Sean Tai
Printed in Canada

McClelland & Stewart,
a division of Penguin Random House Canada Limited,
a Penguin Random House Company
www.penguinrandomhouse.ca

1 2 3 4 5   28 27 26 25 24

Penguin
Random House
McCLELLAND & STEWART

For Daddammi, Ammi, and Amna

CONTENTS

THE KNOT
OF MY
TONGUE

MAJLIS

My daddammi turns the living room into a great book. Before you tell the story, you have to prepare the room for the story. The month of Muharram, I am six years old. Together, we push the furniture to a corner of the room. We spread great white cotton sheets on the ground for the guests. Wall to wall, freshly laundered, stiff and blank like paper. Each wrinkle a giant wave, the entire landscape a perilous journey. I want to run across it. At the front of the room, Daddammi places a chair draped in a black cotton sheet. The seat of the storyteller. A mountain rising at the edge of the sea.

Daddammi tells me to place a glass of water on the ground next to the chair. The storyteller must have water. She will weep. The whole room will weep. I picture what it is to be denied water for three days, to be a girl in the battlefield, to stand and speak before a tyrant with my hands tied. I know how the story goes. I listen to it every day for ten days every year, and every year, it is as if I am there.

Daddammi gives me a pillow covered in black velvet to place on the ground at the front of the room, several steps away from the chair. This is where the marsiya reciter will sit, her book of elegies raised high on the pillow. She will begin the majlis. Women will gather around and recite alongside her. Before the storyteller tells the story of Karbala in speech, it will be recited in verse. Finally, we place some chairs against the wall for the elderly and the pregnant. We are ready.

Bibi Fatimah will come, Daddammi says. The Prophet's daughter will come to our gathering to grieve for her children. I imagine her stepping across centuries, her Arabian mourning robes transforming into the black shalwar kameez of an ordinary Karachi woman attending a majlis in this crowded Urdu-speaking neighbourhood.

You should learn how to recite the majlis, Daddammi says. When the storyteller sits up in the chair, I imagine I am her, that my stories have an unseen listener, and that in the telling, a storyteller summons audiences, speaks the dead into being. Each sound has an ear at the end of it.

Daddammi, are you here? I have something to tell you.

I.

And We made every living thing of water.

*All water has a perfect memory and is
forever trying to get back to where it was.*

—TONI MORRISON

O

At the beginning, not a fall, not clay
    —a deluge.
        Walls, beams, all lines and angles collapse.
                What was vertical
                        drifts horizontal, what was hidden
                                breaks the surface.
Things organize themselves anew,
                        a dream spilling over, all things afloat.
        What was it the poet said?
                Turning and turning,
                        the centre cannot hold.

O

Let me begin again—

        A girl in a windowless room,
        fist sized holes in the walls,
        broken furniture, a closed door.

        The silence before the flood,
        the pressure low and waiting,
        the world a vacuum.

O

all memory is water
        when you touch it   it ripples
when you try to hold it   the words falls apart

O

Let me begin again—

A time of floods, all things wash ashore, polythene
   bags and dying whales, slave ships and nuclear warheads,
anthrax spores and mammoth bones, forgotten names and forgotten bodies
   reveal themselves anew. The earth regurgitates,
gives witness to all things birthed and buried, the old myths, the sleepless
   ancestors, what stood only stood on the crest of a wave.
All things collapse and fall, rock back and forth like a pendulum,
   the boughs of the trees in the breeze sinking and rising, the mountains
never still. When you touch the world, it ripples. When you drop something,
   it comes floating back. When you tell a story, it echoes against itself,
      listening

         —a flood behind a closed door, a girl with her hand at the door.

TONGUE

I pray like Musa: Lord, untie the knot of my tongue
 ease the tightness of my chest, so that I may pour from my tongue

In the desert-thirst beneath the bare sun, Hajar asks her Lord
no water, no sound, no one to call, if I am to die alone here
      what is the use of my tongue?

No words potent enough come to me, my God, I am Maryam
I am not what they think of me. It is not dates I want, but defiance
      sprouting from my tongue

In the court of men, Fatimah of Fadak, the one who never lies
demands—give me what is mine, O men, I will die
      cursing you with the silence of my tongue

Zainab sits in the evening dust by the butchered bodies
  of her brothers and sons—give me rage, give me wailing,
    Lord, show me how to carry this day on my tongue

All language I leave behind in a room, I learn what happens to
     my body is what happens to my tongue

After every defeat, I gather my limbs scattered, I beg fight
    body of mine, the first to desert always is my tongue

Why do I burn? Is this not my inheritance, birthright
    my dowry gift, this art of holding my tongue

Who holds my tongue
      is it you or me who holds my tongue

Fine, here, have it, I don't want it—heat without fire,
                    anger without bite, how it falters, my tongue

Words are wieldier my people insist
                    yet they hold both my fists and my tongue

لسان الحال | THE LANGUAGE WHICH THINGS THEMSELVES SPEAK

unsung tongues   i am unbecome done undone   cipher your decipher
no lung in my tongue   to gone is found in tongue   if you say
something enough times   it loses its meaning   if you don't practise
you forget   i forgot all the names   and now i am a world made of
things   the thing sits inside   the opposite of the thing
the opposite of uncoil is coil   a pencil carrying its own eraser
my mouth holds silence   my mouth holds an underwater language
hunger is gun her   you are a carrier of sound   you are you curled inside
you is a sound that comes after tea   i dream of women around cups of chai
something is only confusing if you try to make sense of it   sue is an anagram
of use   because if it's of no use you can sue   keep wagging your
tongue   till it comes of use   what if i was told the stories all wrong
a mirror of deflections   a poet in a prophet but no profit in poetry   the call
of a prophet is to remember   when i have the mimbar i will remember
stitch water into language   give birth to myself   the tasbih is
for repetition   if you say something enough times
it becomes a part of you   glory glory glory   i say the words until i'm
chewing them   gnawing my maw   a dawning yawn
silence   is a room   after closed doors   the opposite of
silence   is a room   with the walls gone   what if all the words i was
given   are wrong   what if they never take me where i want to go
there are so many places i want to go   what if i am not swimming but
floating   what if i am not floating but sinking   the world
above is all garbled light   beneath the skin of the sea
          i am sound   in   sound alone

REVELATION

In the cave of Hira
where each night Mohammad
disappears into silence
Jibraeel descends with a word
and a command
Recite! & Mohammad cries,
But I am not a reciter! The Prophet and I
know something of wordlessness
of being weak before what
you can never
fully wield
an ocean that can never
fully be yours
revelation birthed
in the lapse of language
an Arabic he cannot touch
the distance between speech
and symbol
between saying and being
between the bang of the cosmos
and the preceding words:
kun faya kun | *Be and it is*
Mohammad falters and Jibraeel
embraces Mohammad
and Mohammad, who cannot read
or write, finds himself speaking in verse
his tongue a flame
lighting shadows in the cave
Recite in the name of the Creator
the most generous, who taught by

the pen, who taught you what
you do not know
and each evening, my mother
whispers the Quran and blows
verses into a glass
of water and I
drink her prayers

LINES

what if I don't want to be postmodern—what if
I don't want fragments but flow—listen, I want
the roaring river, language that shouts—big
type easy print—I don't want clutter but clutter
is another word for hunger—because since his
touch everything became line breaks & caesura
& befores & afters & space & I want continuity
& I am tired of blurs—a steady paragraph & the
focus of a new pair of glasses & sharp clean
circles that declare themselves & to hold on tight
& open my heart wide & only rivers that become
oceans & what is a river that doesn't lead to an
ocean but a line break? dear reader, let me speak
to you plainly—I don't want the metaphor—
I want the name for the thing itself or just give
me the thing & keep the name—dear reader,
sometimes I am sad & that is the only word I
have, but take it, take it, leave me the rest

SAJDAH

the pharaoh was a man who thought he was a god   I know
many such men at the mosque   my prayers are seditious and when I stand
    behind the pharoahs, I curse them
I place my forehead on the ground in sajdah   clay to clay   I collapse
    into the earth

                      sleep a long submission

                        my limbs awaken from groundwater
hungry for the names left behind   a girl searching for her origin story
        a movement

                                    towards the opening

BEGINNING

begin everything with bismillah | in the name of God
reject all idols, say *la ilaha illallah* | there is no god but God

the preacher tells me your husband is your *mijazi khuda* | earthly god

all human beings are equal, but some a degree above others
    so I tell him
    your god is a man is a nation is an idol is an idea
    mine is *rahm*| a womb I begin with and disappear into
qul | say
bism | a name, in the name of which I begin
allah | not a man, not a pronoun, a name, a call, light upon light
ar-rahman | a womb I come from and disappear into
ar-raheem | sound upon sound
    | mercy upon mercy

SAY

in the city square, Maryam addresses the world: *qul* | say
                    wa ja'alna min al ma' kulli shai'in hai | from water is
created every living thing and Hajar takes us to the water, and Zainab
tells us to drink the water, and Yukabid declares: the men needed to
part the sea, but look, the sea is not for drowning it is for carrying, no
passports needed, this is how you let go and this is how you float, and
Hawwa shows us how to rise together instead of always falling, and I
find my words at last, they are growing in the garden of Fatimah, the
one we grew together around cups of chai, the warehouse-turned-
mosque-turned-garden, the one where we speak all day, and our
immigrant tongues become as verdant as soil, and we are full like
we have just come from the ocean, and the red sea folds over itself,
and there are no more partings only arrivals, every day we arrive like
unending spring, see how these women give me words, see how my
tongue moves, do you see?

GARDEN

I am growing a garden and I am going to swallow that garden and from that garden I will grow trees with sentences that flower into delectable phrases and each word is a word I lost and I will pluck it and put it on my tongue and I will plant the seed of each verb to grow and grow and my prayers will be water and my tongue will flower and I will be a forest of overgrown apple trees and juicy persimmons and purple dates and I will be a river and I will rain and I will drink of myself and my stomach will be rich earthy soil where everything keeps growing and I will hold the moon in my mouth and I will be round and full of words that drop like pebbles shining in the night

II.

The language I have learned these forty years,
now I must forgo

Within my mouth you have enjailed my tongue

What is thy sentence then but speechless death,
which robs my tongue from breathing native breath?

—MOWBRAY, RICHARD II

A young man walks the streets of his childhood
        through signs declaring No Dogs or Indians Allowed. A woman turns
one last time from a crowded, desperate train. Millions stumble into
        new-old countries, lines on a map tearing across centuries.
A man and a woman in a refugee camp put down suitcases full of loss,
        look up before they fall asleep to see the same old moon slipping across.

O

A young father sits alone in a parking lot in the middle
        of a Canadian winter for an overnight security job,
wonders if this is what generations of leaving has come to,
        this parking lot, this unforgiving asphalt, these street lamps
swallowing the soundless, sleepless night.

The poet Darwish asks—"where should we go
        after the last frontiers?
where should the birds fly
        after the last sky?"
Shahid writes—"there is a sky beyond
        the sky for me."

In the parking lot, the young father looks up,
        lips remembering lines—

tu shaheen hai parvaaz hai kaam tera
        tere samne asman or bhi hain
sitaron se aage jahan aur bhe hain
        abhi ishq ki inteha aur bhi hain

You are the falcon, to fly is your calling
        there are more skies to come
There are realms beyond even the stars
        further heights for you to ascend

O

In her room, the girl has taken to lying
        on the floor, ear against the ground.
Maybe it is not the sky, Shahid—
        maybe there is more earth
beyond this earth for me.

FORGETTING URDU

the forgetting began in 1858 and long before and everyday since the Redcoats
with their bayonets and bleach began scouring my motherland raw
imperial lather to cleanse the savage. their slogan: Become us but you will never be us.
rinse and repeat. rinse and repeat. rid and repeat. how do i write rebellion
when i can no longer read it? the barbed wire of Angrezi wound around my tongue
bleeds words that are not my own. there is amnesia in my fingers as they trace
my ancestor's verses right to left, alephs and ink tides i can no longer bend
myself into. the parchment will not hold me, tearing when i try to wear its poetry,
rubbing the browning pages against my skin, trying to darken my mouth with
the ink. i swim in these white pages, not cleansed enough, never cleansed enough,
grasping for colour to hold, my tongue falters for words to anchor me,
a washed-out-wreck set adrift without a flag or a call, this cry struggles for sound
ghalib: forgive me, the bows and masts of nastaleeq i have forgotten how to write
i will write a ghazal when اردو returns, carries me and colours me

23

LUCKNOW

how many farewells have you said, lucknow
how many abandonments have you gathered, lucknow

> years of loss: 1857 and 1947, the two great leavings
> the siege, the partitioning, the blood lettings in lucknow

begum hazrat mahal holds her heart in a grave in nepal
commander of 1857, the queen of rebellion flees lucknow

> teach me azadi begum mahal, whisper to me seditious freedom
> tell me of the old days, when the city spat out the invaders in lucknow

1947: my dadi marries my dada as the city breaks around them
amidst the birth of blood and borders, they leave their lucknow

> when she boards the train, she turns her head to say khuda hafiz
> the city shivers, a last tremble before the quiet end of her lucknow

in oxford i find *the indian journals of field marshall lord roberts, 1858*
i unfold his map and wonder which neighbourhood was ours in lucknow

> he writes: *at last the city was cleared of rebels*
> *and we were once more masters in lucknow*

call it rebellion, call it independence, a hush in sikander bagh
do the 2,200 slaughtered sepoys sleep restlessly in lucknow

> begum mahal, the wars never end, the city is hollowing
> old masters always return in new forms to this lucknow

the ghosts of my ancestors wander the city streets in confusion, searching
urdu letters morph into devanagari, urdu becomes english-hindi in lucknow

how many of us have wrenched out our roots, running
i ask my dadi, how many more places to flee since lucknow

this surrender, the crumbling minarets, these pockmarked palaces
how familiar loss has become to you, this evening in lucknow

fresh orders to leave, saffroned men with batons, protests at jumma
these grandmothers i never meet march, claiming the streets of this
lucknow

lucknow then karachi then vancouver—i have many questions, dadi
to which city do i turn of the many lost since lucknow

DEAR BABA

dear baba, you tell me you had to leave, that you cannot speak here,
that in karachi you have a tongue again.

baba, i have been losing words. this morning i woke up and all these
words went missing. baba, what is the word for *longing* in urdu?
baba, teach me how to write my name again.

what about me baba, to where do i run? where is the land that reaches
out, calls me child? where my tongue speaks without betrayal? the
urdu is disappearing, baba, from my mouth and fingertips.

baba, must the children of diaspora find homelands only in poetry,
scattered seeds that will never take root? baba, my generation is
giving up on home as a place of returning. yesterday, a fellow child
of diaspora looked at me through a computer screen, confessed
with red eyes, *you are my home.* baba, maybe we are each other's
homes, maybe that is enough. maybe we hold each other across
oceans and speak tenderness in our broken languages.

dear baba, i have little tolerance for grammar sticklers. it's because
you always asked me to edit your emails, waited every day for me
to come home and check if your response to the craigslist ad was
professional and correct, and i kept telling you it doesn't matter.
don't make it matter.

baba, they never learned our language half as well, not after invasion,
not after plunder, not after centuries of rule. what does it mean to
be finally free? why must we try this hard?

baba, i write in english because it is what i have, but i will break it. i
will break this language, pull it open and tuck in phrases too foreign.
mera wada he. i promise to write bad grammar, not speak all good,
misspell in every email, every school assignment. just for us, baba.

baba, it has been raining for weeks. i wish i could send some to you. i
remember the word for *rain*. barish. *ba rish*. the pause of *ba* as the
monsoon clouds loom. *rish*, relief felt as water kisses parched land.
how the entire city smells like rain. karachi knows the poetry of
rain. how we ran onto the roof, our heads upturned, mouths open
for the first drops. do you remember when chachu sent me an
umbrella from america and i took it to the roof after spotting a
gray cloud? i waited for hours under my american umbrella. i have
never seen anyone use an umbrella in karachi, baba. i wonder if this
has changed or whether the neighborhood children still swarm the
streets, heads skyward, anticipating the first raindrops?

dear baba, what is the word for *des* in English? *nation? homeland?* no,
not quite. english cannot fully know its own erasure. you are my
des, baba. call me when it rains. i remember the word for it. *barish.*
taste of rain on my tongue. barish on my zaban.

HOME, BEFORE THE WAR

—after Warsan Shire

they are calling it
the *European* refugee crisis, she laughs,
they are not the ones drowning
      the Eritrean refugee burns her fingertips with battery acid
      turning her back to the Mediterranean: if they fingerprint
      me i must stay. i need to keep going
where now?
when your passport isn't good enough
and your children have drowned in the Aegean Sea
      i ask her where home is, she tells me
      if you had asked me a few years ago
      i would have said Syria. i am my own home now
the Afghan refugee asks me if she could have
my old phone because hers broke
when she got beat up on West Hastings
      be careful my mother tells me
      don't stand close to the train tracks
      a woman like you was pushed yesterday
go home you fucking terrorist, he spits and drags her
by her headscarf. more of us waking up in the hospital
with improperly stitched up wounds
      in a cafe over lunch: going back means death
      staying here means death. tell me, she demands
      eyes closed, palms on the table, where do i go?
if you could go anywhere, i ask her, where
would you go? home, she says, looking across
the sea. home, before the war

GROCERY SHOPPING

It is June 2015, late afternoon, and you've walked to the Wal-Mart
close to your house. A tall, bulky aging white man with a thick grey
moustache and a sleeveless t-shirt follows you through the automatic
doors. A stack of shopping baskets at the entrance. You reach for
one, pause, deciding on a cart instead. The man is beside you; he picks
up a basket and loudly slams it. You jump from the noise. He's glaring
at you, angry. You don't understand. Maybe you had come in his way?
Is he trying to scare you? You don't understand. You walk away.

You are in the produce section with your cart, looking at croutons
and salad dressings. You sense him before you see him. He pushes you
into the shelves. Your elbow hits metal. He walks. Your arm ringing
like an alarm. You try to speak, sound jostling against tongue. He
hears you. His shoulders high, chin lifted, turns the corner, doesn't
turn around.

You finally move, you wheel your cart around, and around. The
words you manage betray you. Not loud enough, not sharp enough.
You hold your arm, you turn.

In the middle of the canned food aisle, spinning. Hands pale, the cart
hot. Steady, steady. Why were you here? Focus on the labels, letters
blur and swim, your heart in your ears. People walking past you in the
aisles, a box of spaghetti, tomato sauce, a Muslim woman in a hijab,
lost. You don't want anyone to ask you if you need help, to ask if you
are okay, to feel sorry for you, no one, no one gets to have this, no one
gets to make you into a body they think they know how to read.

OLD KABRISTAN

on eid, in the old kabristan we can't find my grandfather's grave
generations of graves sinking and crumbling, crammed together

some with marbled steps, others are mounds of dirt, non-descript
headstones, nastaliq calligraphy, arches and columns and tombs

collapsing under the dirt into each other. we sidestep, walking on
and between mounds and gaps in the earth, dodging the flesh-eating

ants that zip around our feet. in the heat, my mother turns red as
she looks for her father. stray dogs pant beneath the shady tree,

one beneath a marbled canopy. the grave diggers children follow us,
water in repurposed containers to pour onto your loved one's grave

for thirty rupees. my brother holds the bag of rose petals
my mother calls me over, your grandfather's grave is in the same

column as your grandmother, right by this tree. remember it,
she says, meaning I will come here without her. she pours water

onto the thirsty grave, gently digs her finger into the damp earth
my brother and I follow, whispering al-fatiha, and I realize I had

always wanted to do this, to touch the earth and say I come from this

we take turns sprinkling the petals. when we leave there are little holes
on the grave where our fingers had been, drying away in the sun

NUH

When the floods came, I stood at the shore, eyes wide
  to the falling rain, watched the world bleed beyond its lines
the soil erode with silent surrender, the floating mangroves groan and bow
  and all things kneel to the water. And I, a girl, stood
wooden and true, drew myself in solidly, the memory of an ancient banyan
  muscled flanks of wild horses, the bellies of great whales
I knew it was time to build what could carry, to find the high point
  to name what I knew to be the world and carry it with me

III.

But I who am bound by my mirror
as well as my bed
see causes in color
as well as sex
and sit here wondering
which me will survive
all these liberations

—AUDRE LORDE

In the city of empty high rises and immigrant suburbs, the land of
burning rainforests and warehouse mosques, a mother strokes her
daughter's hair, and recites a poem—

millat ke sath
rabta istewar rakh
pewasta reh shajar se
umeede bahar rakh

daughter,
maintain contact
with your people,
stay connected to the tree
and then hope for the spring

O

Are these my people, Zainab asks, the people who did this to me—
        Muhammad, are these your people, tearing apart your family?
This day I cannot carry, listener will you listen, will you take it from me?
        The day I became an exile—not just a city I lost, but my people
        turned from me.

O

Who are my people, the girl asks, where is the tree, and when will it
        be spring?

TWELVE

dollar store mascara   skater shoes a size too big
baguette bags in the latest style   fished out from
the discount bin at Claire's   a period that has yet to arrive

sunday school at the mosque   we flip to the map
in our public school planners   point to the countries we're from
Shazia doesn't want to say   and I can feel her shame

or maybe it is my own   and she points to the country
always in the news   kalanshnikovs and burqas, the place
I am always correcting my school teacher   I am not from

headscarves tied in the latest style   not like the way our mothers do it
hoodies over abayas   sneaking magazines between textbooks
texting Aliya during the urdu majlis   slipping out for an iced capp

sharing headphones with Maryam   who knows how to burn
haram music from the internet   Rihanna, Shakira, Black Eyed Peas
then there's Farah   whose mom is Lebanese

her father is white   lululemon pants and tna hoodies
blonde bangs spilling out   at school she's popular
and Layla   whose mother lets her get waxed

whose sister got her belly button pierced   planning for a tattoo next
the rest of us begging our mothers   to finally go to that salon
where the Iraqi lady   waxes arms, mustaches, eyebrows

in the room in the back   where I run into aunties I know
getting their hair   yanked down by straighteners
or yanked out by a thread   all of us getting ready for the same event

I've got my outfit from Pakistan   ironed on my bed
Eid BBQ in the mosque parking lot   bouncy castle bursting
with kids too big

a stall selling Avon products   henna for 5 dollars per hand
a rack of sequined abayas from Dubai   my mother says
are too expensive

walking barefoot   on the carpeted halls inside
when the prayer hall is empty and   it's just God and me
God, I want to matter   I want to be a writer, I want

to make friends at school   to be loved like the
the girls in my novels   and can we go back to Karachi
next summer?

every time I enter the mosque   the other neighbourhood falls away
the aunties grab my shoulders   they know my name
know my mom   know where I'm from

smack *as salamu alaikum, how are you*   on either cheek
alhamdulillah, how are you?   *alhamdulillah*

IN THE ABSENCE OF THAT GAZE

article by article
let me drag out all these piles
crowding this tiny apartment
let me stretch cables from rooftops of the city's tallest buildings
a thousand pegs I keep for this very day   intimates
flapping in the wind   against glass and cement
    the unwashed declaring
themselves in the sun
      blood ridden   dark
      the bruised the vacant
      bodies into fading ghosts

for all my people
        sister   you too?
        brother   this is the way through
        & this is how I need you

in the absence of that devouring
the windows and doors pushed wide open

the skyline burning in colour today

BROTHERS (I)

—after Sarah M.

at school on Vancouver Island
they called you paki, shit-skin, towelhead
and I wore your anger and your fury
was my fury as I fought off
the bullies shrouded in white—when CSIS came
calling I stood at the door in my hijab
and said fuck off—your fear
my armour—I will not let them touch you
when they deported you
called you terrorist
a threat to national security
spied on you
followed you
put you on no-fly lists
I was there
when they shot at you
while you prayed, I came running
to the reporters and politicians
gathered at the local masjid
I did not complain about
the women's side
that this was the first time
I was allowed to sit next
to you like this because
once again, I was here
and I did not tell them
tomorrow, I will be in the windowless
basement, praying behind the door
with a printout of a helpline

for domestic violence
because brother
I see the game of masculinities
frozen men and women play with you
trying to save us from you
but I stand by you—honour you
stitch your wounds and donate
my blood, give you rhetoric
feed you discourse
my body offers itself to you
my anger, hot words,
feverish op-eds before fajr prayer,
books, Ph.D. theses, law degrees, lawsuits,
petitions, marches, mental health training
I protect you—never call the police
—stuck between you and them
no choice between two violences
when it's you in the bedroom
—your body crushing mine—no one comes
no body before the strike, no petitions,
no articles, no discourse,
no op-eds, no lawsuits, no fury—
a domestic matter, a private matter, a family matter

PHOTOGRAPHS

It's nearing maghrib and I can see the sun setting over
the Karachi skyline, minarets and cement apartment buildings
laundry flapping from latticed windows *karachi ki mashoor hawa*,
Ammi says, Karachi's famous breeze as a gust blows through,
reminding me the sea isn't so far off and how wind travels
on flatter lands. I have been missing mountains lately, but this Karachi breeze,
cool and strong in the heat and traffic, I close my eyes to it, smile as it

sashays past my face. I remember the box of yellowing photographs
of my khalas and phuppos, my aunties with their thin dupattas stylishly
draped around their necks, the breeze hugging their fitted kurtas,
the accents of their curves, thick braids falling down their backs
my uncles with aviator sunglasses and bell bottoms

and there's one with my dadi in the same
breeze, and my dadi's got a firm hold on the folds of her sari,
my mother with permed hair in one, and later, one hand
holding my hand at Quid-e-Azam's mausoleum, and with the other
holding onto her grey chador with the tiny yellow flowers
and my cousin with her dupatta over her head and across
her chest, grinning in film star glasses

and I think of all the things one cannot hold on to—
when the dictator changed and the politics
turned another season, my aunties' clothing
too changed weather

In Quetta Town, just off the highway,
all the men and boys are outside playing cricket before maghrib
I watch a woman, decked in a black chador, she's tugging
at a stubborn goat, trying to bring it inside—
she's the only woman I see. The goat wins and the woman
lets it graze a little longer. The Karachi breeze lifts her chador
    and she holds it down, woman against wind
    that same breeze reaches me and
    I lean into it a little while longer

SUMMER DAY

You never imagined you would use your grandmother's scarf like this.
Tight around the neck. Enough to numb, not enough to kill.

You won't be able to talk about it till you leave him.

A summer day and you're running. he catches you, throws you.
Children play in the park. Your palms burn. The worst thing is to
bring attention to yourself. *Stop* never works.

You pull your headscarf away. You don't want a muslim woman
seen like this. A drunk white man runs up slurring *stop* and now he's
confused, grip slipping.

And then a brown brother runs up and he's pulling the white guy
away, *it's between these two, leave it.* The brother recognizes this scene,
knows it.

You look at the white guy. He has been sleeping rough, on the
streets. *Don't,* he yells. *You can't touch a woman like that.* The brother
backs away, returns to his kids at the swings. he shakes his head at you,
the threat of *later,* stalks off.

The drunk white guy stays. *Do you have anywhere to go?* he slurs, the
stench of alcohol. *Can I get you anywhere?* You don't know how to
answer. You say the first thing. *No, thank you.*

After a while you stopped telling him to stop.
Just to be quiet so the neighbours wouldn't hear.

In the mirror: hands touching arms. Your lips to your own skin. Slip your hand into your other hand, tight. *Aloneness is the stuff of prophethood. Hajar, Maryam, Zainab.* It is warm here, in the years later, the sun shining on your arms, breath alive and full, eyelids heavy like honey.

AFTER THE STORM

after the storm
the window is shattered
a wound pouring sunlight
and you must begin again
set the toppled over chair upright
sweep away the broken glass
place fresh flowers in
a vase at the table
touch the walls
remind yourself
what was the home
I made for myself
what was I to me

BENEATH THE DOME

Light does not work anymore in the same way. What moved

    no longer moves

I behaved like they told me you wanted

    turned into a banner, prayed and waited from the mountain

      What knelt

        is no longer kneeling

the only love I could have was marriage between

        a man and a woman so

I knew how to be good, how to obey. I did everything

        they said you wanted

          my teenage yearning turned into sanctimony

    I followed you into the abyss

        and no one came for me

I want new language, new words

    ochre, green, the hollow base of a tree

I sit beneath the dome and

I cannot find you in the sermon, not anymore

Outside a row of birch trees stir in

the late afternoon breeze

a beam of sun spills through a gap in the branches

pours through the stained windows

washes across the calligraphed walls | الرحمان

and falls onto the carpet before me

You are not in the sermon

not in any of the words I can pull out and fashion. Not a you.

Stop, I want to tell the preacher—   look at this light   pooling before us

US TOO

On the walk to Karbala, the old woman with the cheating husband
tells me you can never trust the love of a man, and my mother
tells me as she finishes her salat, seated on my prayer mat, a tasbih
in hand, beti, in the end we are always alone

One balmy night in Karachi, I lie on my prayer mat
and tell my creator what I want
In the morning my mother finds me and she brings
my body into the warmth of hers, and tells me
beti, I love you. I do not know what to make of these lessons

It wasn't about the cheating husband, why the
old woman turned to me, the turning, what I did not know
then that I do now, when one day I too turn, to women next to me
and say, *look what he did, look what I am*, and they nod, *us too*, and
offer their arms, a canopy of trees that say lean on me a while,
and next, another turning to girls younger, do you know that
you are alone, but also, I am here

BROTHERS (II)

Shaista's brother-in-law is paralyzed from the waist down.

Fawzia Aunty's son lost his eyesight.

My brother after the first day of middle school, sits.

He peels off stickers of stars that he had stuck to his pencil case.

Exchanges his bright orange backpack for a grey one.

His smile for a scowl.

Draws self-portraits with bulging biceps and a six pack.

Mohammed keeps having officers knocking on his door:

So, the Muslim Student Association on your college campus?

Seema's brother enlisted in the American army.

Seema's other brother left the country.

Sibte Jaffer is shot.

Amjad Sabri is shot.

A text: asylum-seeking brother just arrived in London. Shelter? Legal advice.

Ahmed rides his father's motorcycle wearing a glower.

Sakina's father has been missing for two years.

Zainab's brother was gunned down outside their house after a majlis.

I watch Hadi and Yousef shave their beards before the airport.

Noor's uncle's crops drowned in the flood.

Asiya's father lost his job.

Salma's younger brother overdosed behind the mosque parking lot.

When Hanif came out, his parents took away his bedroom door.

My little brother buys a toy gun with his birthday money.

Omar Khadr spent years in Guantanamo Bay as a child.

Fada Mohammed falls in Kabul from an evacuating U.S. Military plane.

My little brother exchanges his softness for a knife between himself
and the world.

My little brother exchanges his softness for a knife between himself
and the world, and I want to say, little brother,

I want a world where you can give up the dagger,

where each day comes running at you, tender and full in colour.

IV.

Unhappy that I am, I cannot heave
my heart into my mouth

——CORDELIA, KING LEAR

Philomela opens her journal and writes—and so I speak without a tongue
          weave words with my fingers from behind the walls of my mouth
I unknot my story that was born in silence, is the kin of silence, knows
          to speak in silence, wombs silence, turns silence into a boat I can oar
Dear sister—I am still here, I am the wind tearing mountains, the bird
          slicing the night, I will tell you what happened—

○

I carry the weight
I carry I drag
I have not touched my skin in years
I might burn
naked primal scribbling
I can't write like I used to
I can't speak like I used to
here in the after
how do I give myself form

O

after the precipice of calamity
at the brink of another morning

after the moonless nights in prison
what was the sky to Zainab
what was the wind   the unobstructed sunlight falling
                              on her hands

○

On a breezy night in Karachi, beneath the soaring alam of an
imambarghah, as worshipers whisper their prayers, children hand out
sweets, and smoke from incense unfurls into the smog-ridden sky, a
woman with a notebook full of handwritten marsiyas has a story to tell—
I could not sing, I could not write, so I went to Zainab in Syria
and wept at her grave, and she gave me back my voice.
Look at my verses. Touch these pages. Look how I
pour. Listen to how my voice carries, liquid as
a flame, watch how it catches—

TWIG

when a twig snaps it loses its bend
      when a twig breaks enough times
it loses all sound
      when you say, here have me because I am
leaving a body hollowing
      a body pushed against the wall
is a place of first snowfall, the sound of
      the heart pushing blood, a moonless
ocean swallowing the night
      the only way to survive is to sleep
is to die a small death each time
      to betray your own body
to lay down your forces
      to bend and blow to the wind
try to touch me
      I am already gone

HAJAR

It was not thirst that drove me to scramble in the desert
    from one hill to the other like a mad pendulum
it was not thirst, not the child crying in the burning sand
    nor my husband's disappearing footsteps
it was that wide, empty horizon that promised no salvation
    all language lost, the sun uninhibited
it was madness, it was reaching the end of the world and needing
    to hear my feet against the ground, my breath ragged
my heart thundering against the silence of the barren earth
    I was not looking for water, I wanted evidence of my own life

HERON

this morning you saw a heron standing
     in the flooded canal   still   that gaze you recognize
at age ten   in the coast mountains   astonished
     stars spilling across a dark sky   a single audience
before the galaxy or standing before the endless ocean expanding
     with the shoreline   steady   rounding like
the horizon   something inside you sinking to its knees
     or perhaps the heron is speechless   perhaps it is not awe
but terror   or what happens after terror
     perhaps the heron   wide-eyed and motionless
is lost inside herself   not engrossed
     but dazed   perhaps she can't remember how she got here
perhaps she is letting go   perhaps she has not yet
     realized she has gone astray   and this is the moment
before she begins   tracing the outline of the wound
     the distance between the different ways   a body goes quiet
the movement of sound and shape   she finds when she reaches
     the margins   out beyond this moment
out beyond this room   out beyond his hands
     he flings you across the room   your body can do that
can be flung   flight   fight
     or freeze to be frozen   you are thinking of hikers
found beneath mountain avalanches   in blocks of ice
     eyes shut   or wide open   you know what it is
to be   in frozen time

MARSIYA

I.

A setting sun stretches
across splayed bodies, a river sieged
a caravan surrounded, the desert scorched
no water for days, how hands
become knives, how history turns
and tears itself

II.

The quiet after a slaughter
the air thick and metallic
a woman searching a massacre
my Hussain, my brothers, my sons,
is this small mound of earth
my Asghar

III.

Gray-haired, bereft Zainab
grabs her veil as the tents catch fire
run, she commands
she grabs the children she can, *where is Sakina?*

IV.

(& Hussain, for whom Mohammad prolongs his sajdah when the child
climbs his back like a horse rider, who travels Madina hanging from
the shoulders and arms of prophethood)
(& Ali Akbar whose smile is the smile of Mohammad, whose voice
carries the lilt of Mohammad, whose adhan ascends like Mohammad's,
whose sweet tooth is as indomitable as Mohammad's, whose hair curls
in the way Mohammad's curled)

V
How we are driven from city to city
exiled among our own. Hussain, wake up.
get up, Abbas. Grandfather, look what has become of us

VI.
In the day's last light,
beneath the dying drumbeats
of war and victory, a women gathers
familiar limbs, a child holding another child, crushed
beneath the boots of raiding soldiers

VII.
My son, you who would rise
at a single call, now despite
my pleas, my son,
not a breath of yours stirs for me

VIII.
A girl, asleep against a body,
her graying aunt shakes her, wake up child,
have some water. she stirs, they tore my earrings
they burned my clothes, but I found him
'ammati, I found my father

IX.
A woman stands guard
in the open desert
brandishing a tree branch
against soldiers and carrion birds
not the dark I fear
but what moves towards me

X.

In the widening descent of night,
the sound of a mother's wail,
pouring sand into hair, forehead in the dirt
how do I carry this
let the sun never rise
let there be no tomorrow

I HAVE NEVER SEEN MY DADDAMMI CRY,
EXCEPT AT THE MAJLIS

My daddammi does not cry when she tells me about Rana, the first
child she buries. A train ride through blood and borders, a husband
she is just getting to know. Twin new-borns cry at her, Rana and
Shabana, a rhyming couplet. No woman to turn to in this new country,
she teaches herself how to mother, how to hold a child to her breast.
Rana begins to fade into illness, and my daddammi, a girl, does not
know how to make her new-born live.

My daddammi tells me about Anwar, the second child she buries.
The adolescent country, the power outages, her eighteen-year-old.
She waves a fan to her face in the heat, the electricity has been gone
all day. Anwar makes her a cup of chai. He whistles. Let me see if I
can do something with the cables, he goes to the rooftop, whistling.
The sky begins to rain, and in the water and the flash of light, Anwar
falls. My daddammi waiting for him. My daddammi after the hospital,
after the calls, in the stillness of maghrib, finds the chai, unfinished,
she freezes it, scrapes out a teaspoon of it each day.

My daddammi tells me about Shabana, the third child she buries.
The cancer at Shabana's throat, her children grab on to their mother.
The last days in the hospital stretch, her daughter heaving for breath.
My daddammi at the mosque, sits by the alam, and asks Allah to ease
her child's fight. Picks up her daughter's children, holds them to her
chest, teaches them how to open their hands and let go.

Daddammi is at the majlis. I sit by her feet in a gathering of mourners.
The storyteller says Zainab, says Karbala. My daddammi takes out her
handkerchief, places it on her eyes, that old story sweeps into her, her
shoulders part, and she, like a river, pours and pours and pours.

WHEN ZAINAB RETURNS

translated from Munshi Chunnal Dilgeer's marsiya "Ghabrai gi Zainab"

what will she find
when Zainab returns
when she calls out their names

at the door she will stand
how these once crowded rooms
have now fallen still

—no Qasim
no Abbas, no Akbar anywhere—
no Aun, no Muhammad,
where to turn for Asghar

the neighbours will ask
what happened to your arms
what is this bruise—to how many people
will she have to explain the burn
of the rope around her wrists

what more will she find
when Zainab returns home

GRASS

the quivering green centre
fresh   supple
a bolt of vivid green
solitary   shivering in the wind
electric persistence in
a tornado eye
you are the blade in the ground
rooted to the planet
look: this jagged sharpness
this self-will
this dogged survival

V.

Even so, this fear will not leave you
That though I cannot speak
I can still walk

—KISHWAR NAHEED

So eat and drink, and let your eyes be refreshed.
But if you see any of the people, say, 'I have vowed silence to
The Merciful, so I will not speak to anyone today.'

—QURAN 19:26

My peace is in my aloneness.

—RABI'A AL-BASRI

Turning and turning, a woman in exile tells a story. The story spreads.

○

Centuries later, after the fall of one tyrant and the rise of many more, a journey of three days by foot, beginning at an ancient graveyard where Babylonian prophets lie next to the dead of the Iraq war, a river of pilgrims in mourning attire walk north towards the Euphrates.

Once a desert massacre, the land narrates itself like rain remembering ancient lakebeds—here Abbas lost his arms. Here Akbar was slain. Here lies Asghar. And here, Zainab's children. This is the water they were refused. This is the hill from which Zainab saw the slaughter of her brother. This is where the tents stood before they were lit on fire. Here the women became roped to camels headed west, watched the land disappear from the horizon.

○

The girl walks into the story, follows the river. Are these my people? Is this the tree?

○

Here is the room. Unventilated, the blinds drawn. There are three fist-sized holes at various spots on the bedroom walls. The standing mirror cracked, jagged lines shooting out from the place of contact. The desk chair broken. The door of the used wardrobe the girl found for him has a long, splintering crack at its centre.

She opens her mouth, the sentences turn against her, slip and float away. What is the language of water and air? How to speak in blank space and line breaks?

And then in the morning before she showers, a bruise on her arm from the night before, the shape of his nails pressing in, evidence of a body tearing into another. Takes a photo of it, holds it still. She stands under the shower and touches   arm.   Hot water hits   skin. and arm becomes   *my arm*   and body becomes   *my body*
    limbs and skin and sinews at the mercy of   *my decision*

O

On the road to Karbala, next to the Euphrates, gentle hands offer plates
of steaming food, water, tea.

   A mother from Awamiyya arrives with a photograph of her son for
   anyone who will stop to listen, *they killed him, he was jameel, he was*
   beautiful.

A woman confesses over a plate of chicken and rice—my husband
left me for a younger woman and now I come here every year.
She pats the space next to her, come sit down.

   A Hazara woman folds a page of her prayer book and falls asleep
   against a wall at the shrine. Sunlight slips through the courtyard,
   across her face, her arms, her feet.

O

What was it the poet said, hum dekhenge—

      we shall witness   certainly we too shall witness
            that day which has been promised   written on slate
      when the mountains of tyranny   shall blow away like cotton
            and beneath our feet, the feet of the silenced
                  the earth will drum like a beating heart

⸲

◯

The girl steps into the flood. The old stories rise, reassemble—

burning feet   parched tongue
        Hajar

                not even Ibrahim   Hajar
at the beginning   at the direction of every prayer
        with the rising and setting sun
                        not circling but circled
Hajar in the desert
        the earth splitting open
                zamzam cool and shining at her feet

Yukabid   stands between the river and the tyrant
        chooses the river   surrenders her child to the Nile
                and between her and the tyrant
        twice, the river chooses her

Maryam with birth pangs
        in the outskirts of a town
                where the people slander her
conceives a story   without the need of any man
        alone with a date palm that bends towards
                what is its own

Zainab alone dragging her family
                out of burning tents   Zainab in the caliph's palace
        tongue aflame   Zainab
                returning home   to empty rooms
        the same story   again again
        Zainab   splitting open a language
                you can walk inside

qul | say

      the god of Hajar

      the theology of the abandoned

          each tradition   a thread

               unspooling

                    with a woman alone

O

Here she is oceans away from the room where it happened.
There's the wall behind the door, next to the wardrobe,
                    only accessible when the door is closed—
                    where pinned, she fell into silence.
                    And there, the bed, where the sentences fled.
        She and the door meet.
        She keeps walking.
        She walks continents away, the desert sky shadows her
footsteps in this old story—for hundreds of years she won't need to
say a word.

WUDHU

after Mohja Kahf

the first thing the founder does
is look for water

my palms cup water
to make clay malleable

before the dawn prayer
I pour water over my face

flush it around in my mouth and out
wet hands trace right arm then left arm

find an opening between hair
and touch moisture to clay

limbs bend over themselves
fingers slide over toes

each morning I build my body anew
coax these bones and sinews

to settle into a self
to bend and bow without breaking

LOOK WHAT I HAVE FOUND HERE, MOTHER, THE THING FARTHEST FROM LONELINESS

Far from home
in the city of quads and cloisters,

I find Zunaira in the room next to mine
she a mix of English and Urdu like me

I have not told anyone yet that story I have been carrying
the one without any words. Each day from my dorm room

I wait for the sound of her return, her boots on the steps
the jangle of her keys, her door creaking open

I pop my head in the hallway, call out to her
bring two cups of chai, lie in her bed

From beneath her covers, I watch her
wipe off makeup in the evening light

her feet on her dresser, pink and white
striped pyjamas, tired gentle lines around her eyes

when she smiles at me. We talk about the day
and sip our chai and I want to tell her

how she has been saving me.
She tells me about the obnoxious Americans

at the formal, the guy standing too close
the bland British food, how her feet hurt

and then in the night, the moon at the window
when our conversations have settled themselves

she joins me under the covers
shoulder to shoulder

and we bare to each other what
we terribly want from the world

and convince the other she will find it,
hold it, and want so badly for her life

to be kind to her, and my tongue
feels like mine, and my words feel like mine

and I have a story to tell her.
She holds my hands under the covers

and then, all nerves, I laugh after I tell
her the story, shoulders melting with relief,

I say, someday I'm going to write a poem
about this, because it is all a poem,

that another woman can be a homecoming,
that these conversations with her are what I have been searching—

time bends and holds all of both of us.
She laughs and says yes, you better write a poem about me

and I say, yes, of course, because is poetry
not the language best suited for love?

BECOMING

you know the earth in winter
    the dry root
you know what it is to shrivel
        to fall
and yet look how these trees persist
    look how you become a tree
how you gather the words left behind
    assemble them from the scatter
        plant them under your tongue
           to stay
from where the frost has taken root
    how you melt
        into spring
let philosophies long dormant
    emerge
    take root and grow
        brave and expansive
you gather and open and pour
    fresh layer of tree bark
        renewed limbs
           petalled and tender
you find yourself at the swell
    a place of mutable edges
        rivers flooding
           boundaries collapsing
look how you earth
    another kind of stillness
        another kind of spring
        not broken
    but becoming

A POEM FOR THE SIXTEEN-YEAR-OLD READING IN THE DARK

—after Adrienne Rich

I want to make you laugh
      You standing there by the window
          next to the day's dying light
              a book in hand hungry for a line

    something to pull
               something to set afloat

Come, let us go for a walk. I fashion you shoes
cover you in a wool coat   here's a scarf
          twirl you around in a meadow and grab both your hands

Listen, God is not something you have to fight for
          It is here. You have already arrived. It is yours

You don't have to beg. You don't have to lie in bed waiting

You can look away from the wall
      Watch how the river melts and roars down a mountain
Watch how it sighs into the sea

Look at the lines on your palms
      A map. The destination: always *here*
You are not shameful. You are not alone, but you are, but that is okay,
  I promise

There are dead leaves from last fall still
        clinging to the tree that now unfurls with new leaves
                There are wild salmon thrashing up a mountain stream
a whale and her calf in the cold northern seas

There is you by the window with a poem in your hand
        an ache you cannot name

Listen, I want to tell you
        it's true, nothing remains the same, no skin cell, no
same butterfly wing, no eggshells with the same spots
even the ancient are always dying
                even the moon shifts in her sleep

When you put down the book, it will be another room
        another light and you too will stir and the words will come to you

PRELUDE: THE STORY OF KARBALA

It is a centuries-old story set in the land of ancient Babylonian prophets by the river Euphrates, retold in gatherings every year in the Islamic month of Muharram, traveling across continents and languages.

In 680 AD, Hussain, the grandson of the Prophet Muhammad and the son of Mohammad's daughter Fatimah, leaves his hometown of Medina with his family. It has been fifty years since the death of Muhammad and the community is in turmoil. The Umayyads have the caliphate and Yazid, who is widely considered to be a tyrant and unfit to rule, has taken the seat of power. In the years to come, he will lead attacks on the sacred city of Mecca, raiding homes, killing families, and setting the Ka'aba on fire. Yazid seeks allegiance from the Prophet's family. Hussain and the family refuse.

Unsafe in the city of their grandfather, the family and a small group of their closest supporters set out on a journey east, across the desert towards Kufa where the people have promised support. En route, close to the river Euphrates, in a place called Karbala, Yazid's army intercepts the family. Thousands of soldiers surround the small caravan and block all access to water. Support from Kufa never comes. Family members attempt to push through the soldiers and bring back water. No one returns from the river. *Death with dignity is better than a life of humiliation*, says Hussain, still refusing to submit. Over the course of an afternoon, on the 10th of Muharram—Ashura day—the army kills Hussain and most of the men in the caravan. Zainab, Hussain's sister, takes charge over the surviving members of the family, who are are all imprisoned and taken to Damascus in shackles, their tents and belongings set on fire. At the court in Damascus, when Yazid brings out the prisoners to parade them in front of the courtiers, Zainab steps forward, her wrists bound together, head high: *O Yazid, I swear by Allah that I consider you to be too low and not fit even to be reprimanded and reproached, but what am I to do*—she begins, publicly berating the caliph and the community for their violence and betrayal. Eyes lower with embarrassment, feet shuffling, murmurs and movements of assent in the crowd. Yazid stumbles.

In exile, Zainab organizes gatherings to lament and narrate again and again what happened to her family in Karbala. She calls the people to witness her mourning, to mourn alongside her, to participate in remembering. Her story begins to spread throughout the Muslim lands. A lifetime is not enough for Zainab's story, the fall of a single empire is not enough, the end of Yazid is not enough—it spills across generations and through centuries, calling, taking on different colours and banners, offering words for gatherings of loss, of resistance, for those in need of a language that knows survival.

Poems containing Quranic references and translations by the poet are based on and amended from the following texts:

—Bakhtair, Laleh. *The Sublime Quran: English Translation*. Kazi Publications. 2007
—Cowan, and Hans Wehr. *A Dictionary of Modern Written Arabic*. Ithaca: Cornell University Press. 1966

The line "turning and turning, the centre cannot hold" is a reference to "The Second Coming" by W.B. Yeats.

The lines "growing in the garden of Fatimah, the one we grew together around cups of chai" is an ekphrasis of Shazly Khan's painting "My tea party in paradise."

The line "where should we go after the last frontiers? where should we go after the last skies?" in Section II is from Mahmoud Darwish's poem "The Earth is Closing on Us", discovered as an epigraph in Agha Shahid Ali's poem "Ghazal" in *Rooms Are Never Finished* (2002). The quote "there is a sky beyond the sky for me" is from Shahid's version of Darwish's poem "Eleven Stars," titled as "Eleven Stars Over Andalusia" in the same book.

The couplets "tu shaheen hai parvaz hai kaam tera" in Section II are from a ghazal by Muhammad Iqbal, translated by the author.

"Home, before the war" is written after Warsan Shire's poem "Conversations About Home."

The lines "Millat ke sath rabta istewar rakh . . ." in Section III are from Muhammad Iqbal's poetry collection *Bang-e-Dara* (1924), translated into English in the following stanza.

"Twelve" is written after Fatimah Asghar's poem "If They Come For Us" and Safia Elhillo's poem "Ode to My Homegirls."

"Brothers (I)" is written after Sarah M who performed a poem titled "Brown brother" in 2015.

The poem "after the storm" is written after Maulana Rumi.

Stanza VII of the poem "Marsiya" is a translation of lines from Mehshar Lacknavi's Urdu noha "Haye Haye Ali Akbar." Marsiyas and nohas are elegies and lamentations about the events of the Battle of Karbala recited in gatherings called the majlis.

"When Zainab Returns" is translated by the author from Munshi Chunnal Dilgeer's 19th Century Urdu marsiya "Ghabrai gi Zainab."

"Grass" is written after Kishwar Naheed's Urdu poem, "Ghans to mujh jesi he."

The first epigraph in Section V contains an excerpt from Kishwar Naheed's poem "Anticlockwise" translated from Urdu to English by Rukhsana Ahmed in her book *We Sinful Women: Contemporary Urdu Feminist Poetry* (The Women's Press Ltd. 1991).

The lines that start with "hum dekhenge / we shall witness" in Section V are a translation of the opening section of Faiz Ahmed Faiz's Urdu poem "Hum Dekhenge," originally published as "Va Yabqa Vajhu Rabbika" in *Mere Dill Mere Musafir* (Shaheen Book Centre 1982).

The lines "the first thing the founder does is look for water" in "wudhu" are from Mohja Kahf's poem "The First Thing" from her collection *The Hagar Poems* (University of Arkansas Press 2016).

"A poem for the sixteen-year-old reading in the dark" is written after XIII (Dedications), the last section from Adrienne Rich's poem "An Atlas of the Difficult World."

"Prelude: the Story of Karabala" is based on *The Origins and Early Developments of Shi'a Islam* by S. H. M. Jafri, *A Probe Into the History of Ashura* by Ibrahim Ayati, *One Drop of Blood* by Ismat Chughtai, "Karbala: A History of the House of Sorrow" by Agha Shahid Ali, and oral retellings of the story in community gatherings (majlis).

ACKNOWLEDGEMENTS

The following authors and their words shaped my thoughts during the writing of this book:

Leah Horlick's *For Your Own Good*
Agha Shahid Ali's *Rooms Are Never Finished*
M. NourbeSe Philip's *She Tries Her Tongue, Her Silence Softly Breaks*
Toni Morrison's essay "The Site of Memory"
Mohja Kahf's *Hagar Poems* and *Western Representations of Muslim Women*
Rukhsana Ahmed's *We Sinful Women: Contemporary Feminist Urdu Poetry*

Thank you to the editors of the following publications in which versions of poems in this manuscript first appeared: *The Capilano Review, Contemporary Verse 2, Minola Review, Room, Writers' Trust RBC Bronwen Wallace Award 2021, Tin House, Living Hyphen,* and *PRISM.*

My deep gratitude to my editor, Canisia Lubrin, who first received this manuscript in a vastly different shape, recognized where it was trying to go, believed in it, and helped it arrive. Thank you for approaching each line with care, attention, heart, generosity, and wisdom. For showing me the long and necessary work of crafting language that can move beyond patriarchal and colonial tongues. Learning from you has made me a better poet.

I am immensely grateful to Kelly Joseph, without whom this book would have never been finished. Thank you for leading me through the confusing process that is a writer's first book with skill, kindness, patience, and the utmost thoughtfulness. Thank you for being with me and this book at every step.

Thank you also to Stephanie Sinclair, Talia Abramson, Blossom Thom, the designers, typesetters, and the entire the team at McClelland & Stewart.

Thank you to friends, mentors, teachers, colleagues, and readers who have held poems from this manuscript at various stages through the years and have offered support—both emotional and literary—at different turns: Afrin Shairaj, Sana Naeem, Nikita Azad, Michelle Jia, Deborah Campbell, Léa Taranto, Amber Dawn, Sheryda Warrener, Rahat Kurd, Nayani Jensen, Sarah Munawar, Melissa Godin, Tabia Yapp, Safia Elhillo, Cicely Nicholson, Irfan Ali, and Leah Horlick.

Thank you to Rahat who first suggested that I had a book project at hand and then witnessed it take shape.

Thank you Deborah, for your friendship, mentorship, life-changing counsel, letters, conversations, and for more than I can ever write here.

Thank you to the women on Albert Street. Living with you changed me, changed my writing and helped me find the words after I had walked away: Zunaira, Katongo, and Sana.

Thank you also to Chiyi Tam, Krishnendu Ray, Jelani Munroe, Sepideh Khazei, Tasha Kim, Masooma Hussain, Aaliya Ali, Fatima Al-Samak, and Sarah Al-Samak.

Baba, thank you for showing me how to cultivate the ingredients vital for a life free and open to poetry. Ammi, thank you for the gift of shayari, for embodying shayari, and for everything else—you are on every page. My beautiful, tender-hearted brothers, Hyder and Jawad. Amna, for not caring *log kya kehenge,* for showing me how—this is for you.

Thank you foremost to Zikri. For telling me I could do it and then making it possible, for your Arabic translations, for stopping everything to patiently listen to every new version of every line in this book. For giving me the courage I needed to tell this story.

ZEHRA NAQVI is a Karachi-born writer raised on unceded Coast Salish Territories (Vancouver, BC). She is a winner of the 2021 RBC Bronwen Wallace Award for Emerging Writers awarded by the Writers' Trust of Canada. Her poem "forgetting urdu" was the winner of *Room's* 2016 Poetry Contest. Zehra has written and edited for various publications internationally. She holds two M.Sc. degrees in migration studies and social anthropology from Oxford University where she studied as a Rhodes Scholar. *The Knot of My Tongue* is her debut poetry collection.